Shattered Dreams?

GOD HAS NOT ABANDONED YOU

Dawn M. Mitchell

TRILOGY CHRISTIAN PUBLISHERS

TUSTIN, CA

Trilogy Christian Publishers
A Wholly Owned Subsidiary of Trinity Broadcasting Network
2442 Michelle Drive, Tustin, CA 92780

For information, address Trilogy Christian Publishing

Rights Department, 2442 Michelle Drive, Tustin, Ca 92780.

Trilogy Christian Publishing/ TBN and colophon are trademarks of Trinity Broadcasting Network.

For information about special discounts for bulk purchases, please contact Trilogy Christian Publishing.

Manufactured in the United States of America

Trilogy Disclaimer: The views and content expressed in this book are those of the author and may not necessarily reflect the views and doctrine of Trilogy Christian Publishing or the Trinity Broadcasting Network.

10 9 8 7 6 5 4 3 2 1

Library of Congress Cataloging-in-Publication Data is available.

ISBN 978-1-64773-038-3

ISBN 978-1-64773-039-0

Contents

To my wonderful husband, John,
who makes me feel like a "princess" every day
and loves me always.

ox

Acknowledgements

My health may fail, and my spirit may grow weak,
but God remains the strength of my heart; he is mine forever.
Psalm 73:26

To my Lord Jesus: Thank You for being the strength of my heart, for Your love, Your mercy, and Your presence always. Writing this book has been an eye-opening experience and I am grateful for the opportunity You have given me to do so. Thank You for the doors You have opened, the doors You have closed, and enlightening me to the blessings You bring through difficult situations.

To my husband: Thank you for supporting me in every way to make all my dreams and wishes come true. You are an amazing husband and I love you.

To Gina: You are more like a sister than a friend, and I have been blessed by your friendship tremendously over the years. You have an ability to help me try things that I didn't think I could do, and for that, I am grateful. You have made my life better, and at times more adventurous. Thank you for always being there, for listening, sharing, and keeping me grounded.

To Mom: This has been just as difficult for you as it has for me. Thank you for listening and praying.

And to Ruthie: Thank you for being a part of everyday life. ox

Foreword

"Oh, taste and see that the Lord is good; blessed is the man (or woman) who trusts in Him!" (Psalm 34:8 NKJV) Trust is the firm belief in the reliability of someone or something. The Word says that we are "blessed" when we trust in Him. Yet, why do we struggle with trusting Him? Is it because we've placed our trust in ourselves or others and we/they have failed? Or is it because there is often a wait time that goes along with trusting that is too hard? We don't like to wait; it's not in our DNA. We order fast food because it is just that, "fast" food. Trust carries us through some of the darkest times while we wait for God to answer. But what happens when His answer isn't what we asked for? These are the times our trust is tested the most. We must "choose" who we are going to trust. Trust in Him! He will never fail you.

No matter what you are facing there is a God who loves you. As you read the following pages, I pray that you will allow God to speak to you and bring healing. Healing comes in many different forms. I've seen this in Dawn's life. Healing, or an answer to prayer, doesn't always come immediately, nor in the way we anticipate or expect. This, too, is revealed within the pages of this book.

Writing this forward comes as an honor and privilege, as I have walked this road beside my friend. I vividly remember the phone call and those first few hours after she found out she had lost her baby and dealing with the lingering hurt that accompanied the miscarriage.

Through the pages of this book, Dawn portrays the raw emotions that surfaced as she walked through this trial and the years of infertility that followed.

This book has been part of the healing process for my friend. As I reread it, the tears flowed as I recall the moments as though they were yesterday. Dawn has walked a road that many couples have walked and yet, for various reasons, others will not openly talk about the loss and ensuing pain. When we hear of an acquaintance or co-worker having a miscarriage, we usually walk around the topic without bringing it up, so we don't upset the individual.

If you know someone who is struggling with broken and shattered dreams, then I highly recommend this book. It is written by someone who has walked this road and learned a lot about trusting God along the way. It is the candid and firsthand experience of a woman who is not only my friend but also a mom. She will one day get to meet her baby in Heaven.

Taste and See that the Lord is good. May these words and those that are written in this book strengthen your faith and help you to trust Him regardless of what you may be facing.

Blessings,
Gina
Friend and Pastor's Wife

DAWN M. MITCHELL

Introduction

Growing up, I always knew I would have a houseful of children. I loved children. I began babysitting at age twelve. Yes, that may seem young, but my mother was right down the street. While my teenage friends worked at the local mall or restaurants, I spent my summers and weekends working as a nanny. I was fortunate to work for one family at a time, and I was with each family for two years or more. It was wonderful...and heartbreaking when the job was over.

In my wildest dreams, it never occurred to me that my husband and I would struggle with infertility and miscarriage. I felt my dreams were shattered, laying in tiny little pieces all around me. The longer it went on, the more broken and out of place I felt.

Crazy as it sounds, I also felt embarrassed. Embarrassed because my body didn't work right, and out of place because we didn't have children and it seemed everyone around us did. It seemed so easy for everyone else. I felt ashamed to share my story. I felt like people really didn't want to hear the story of the girl who couldn't conceive, who couldn't carry to term. It's a downer, I get it.

But my story is part of what makes me who I am. Second Corinthians 1:4 says: "He comforts us in all our troubles so that we can comfort others. When they are troubled, we will be able to give them the same comfort God has given us." As we go through difficult times and God brings strength and peace to us, we will be able to bring comfort to others in similar situations. We will understand how they feel because we have been where they are.

I learned there are other people like me, who are trying to sift through the broken pieces of a dream shattered. The shattered dream you're facing doesn't have to be infertility and miscarriage, it could be anything from job loss, to prison, to bankruptcy, to foreclosure on your home, sickness, the loss of a spouse, or even difficulties with your children.

The pain and emotions a person go through when facing any difficult situation all have similarities. My prayer for you is that my situation and the things I have learned will bring comfort, peace, and insight into your own struggles, and bring you closer to God; encouraging you to lean on and trust Him.

Don't ever believe the lie of the enemy and let yourself feel ashamed or unworthy because life isn't progressing as you imagined. Usually, that is the time we become the closest to God.

I can assure you, whatever battle you are facing, God will not abandon you and life does go on. He will help you sift through the ashes to see the beauty, and you will find blessings through your shattered dreams.

DAWN M. MITCHELL

To all who mourn in Israel, he will give a crown of beauty for ashes, a joyous blessing instead of mourning, festive praise instead of despair. In their righteousness, they will be like great oaks that the Lord has planted for his own glory.

Isaiah 61:3

Prologue

Dear Anna,

Over the years, I have really struggled with you not being here, and not feeling like a mom. God gives so many women babies and when those babies leave is His choice. He creates all things and creates us in His image. ("So God created human beings in his own image. In the image of God he created them; male and female he created them. Genesis 1:27)

We were made by Him and for Him. ("For through Him God created everything in the heavenly realms and on earth. He made the things we can see and the things we can't see—such as thrones, kingdoms, rulers, and authorities in the unseen world. Everything was created through him and for him." Colossians 1:16)

We are made to glorify God in word and deed but are reminded our days are numbered. ("Lord, remind me how brief my time on earth will be. Remind me that my days are numbered—how fleeting my life is. You have made my life no longer than the width of my hand. My entire lifetime is just a moment to you; at best, each of us is but a breath." Psalm 39:4-5)

As short as your life was, God created it with a purpose. That purpose, in ways I may or may not ever realize, will ultimately bring Him glory. I trust God that you fulfilled the purpose He created you for, and then He called you home. I love you.

> Until we meet again,
> And with all my love,
> Mommy

Plans and Desire

I prayed for this child, and the Lord has
granted me what I asked of him.
1 Samuel 1:27

John and I began dating in high school. It's fun to say you are married to your high school sweetheart and I feel blessed to be able to say so. We feel like we grew up together, we had been friends for two years prior to dating. He was at my house often and would walk the dog with me. I loved those uninterrupted summer nights. We would talk about our dreams for the future—moving to a house in the country out of state, what kind of dogs we wanted, having kids. Thinking back on this now it makes me laugh a bit because I think we named the dogs and the kids! When you're dreaming, everything works out just as you planned.

But notice the last three words in the previous sentence: "as you planned." At that time, our dreams did not take into consideration the plans God had for us.

We both accepted Jesus as our Savior and surrendered our hearts, and lives, to Him on Labor Day weekend in 1990, but we did not fully understand the need to also submit our plans and desires to Him as well.

We married after college. When I landed my first job as a Dental Hygienist, we moved out of state and purchased our first home in the beautiful mountains of Virginia. It was a small, three-bedroom rancher about two-thirds the way up the mountainside. It was in a beautiful area just outside a charming little town. Soon, a Golden Retriever/Collie mix needing a home showed up at our front door. He was about six months old and had been dumped off at the home of someone else who lived on the mountain. They did not want him and just let him go to fend for himself. He was as sweet as could be and a perfect fit for us. God was allowing our dreams to become reality. Marriage—check. Moving to the country—check. Jobs—check. House—check. Dog—check. Baby...mmm—not yet.

We decided to enjoy married life a bit and get settled before having children. We had lots of time for that. Our one-year wedding anniversary came and passed, and we felt it was time to begin a family. It never occurred to us that we might not conceive immediately.

Two-and-a-half years later, we were over the moon to find out we were finally expecting our first child.

Funny how much more it seems you appreciate something when you have to wait for it.

Then we started wondering—would we be good parents? Would we be able to provide? What about daycare? After all, our family was in Baltimore. I think all first-time parents have the same questions, you want to be the best parent and provider you can for your child.

Saying we were excited is an understatement. After two-and-a-half years we were overjoyed and just could barely believe it was going to happen. God had answered our prayer and was allowing us to have a child, a child He created and planned for. It was fun to start a baby name list and pick up little this and that's—a baby carriage, handmade sweaters—and reading the book: *What to Expect When You're Expecting*. Baby stuff. We tried to keep it to ourselves until we were farther along in the pregnancy. Well, that did not last long. We told our parents, our siblings, my best friend, Gina, and maybe a few church people. Good news, right? Who can resist? A testimony of God answering prayer.

It is strange, because all along I had this nagging feeling, an unease about the pregnancy. I kept blowing it off as first-time pregnancy jitters since it took so long to conceive. It never actually occurred to me that I would not carry to term; there was just this...feeling. I kept reminding myself this pregnancy was in God's timing. He is the giver of life and brought this forth at the time He chose.

At seven weeks I had some spotting and went to see the doctor. She assured me that this sometimes happens and there is usually nothing to be concerned about. But to put me at ease, she sent me to the local hospital for an ultrasound since her tech had left for the day. We were able to not only see the baby but to hear the heartbeat for the first time. Watching and hearing the heartbeat on the monitor, we were mesmerized and instantly fell in love with this tiny growing baby. The nurse said at seven weeks the heartbeat is not often heard. We heard it loud and clear. Everything seemed to be okay, so we went home, amazed at having had our first glimpse of our child.

Although everything was fine, I found it difficult to shake the strange feeling I had. Was it a feeling of dread? Anxiety? First time pregnancy jitters? I was not confident I would carry to term. "Fearful" is a better word. I prayed. I prayed for the baby, the pregnancy...I watched for signs of continued pregnancy...or lack of it. I just could not shake that uneasy feeling.

"For just as the heavens are higher than the earth, so my ways are higher than your ways and my thoughts higher than your thoughts" (Isaiah 55:9).

I wanted this child so badly and the feeling, the thought of it not happening, was almost crushing. I worried. I prayed again and again for a healthy pregnancy and a healthy baby. James 5:16 states,

> Therefore, confess your sins to one another [your false steps, your offenses], and pray for one another, that you may be healed and restored. The heartfelt and persistent prayer of a righteous man (believer) can accomplish much [when put into action and made effective by God—it is dynamic and can have tremendous power]. (AMP)

That was not what I was doing. I was persistent; persistently pleading *my* case. I was pleading for *my* hopes, *my* wills, *my* desires. Not once did I stop long enough to breathe and dare to ask His desire and plan.

Herein lies one of the lessons I learned. It is okay to have our own hopes and dreams, but we should always seek His will and His plan first. Our plans and desires should fall under His if we want to be truly happy and content in this life. His ways are not our ways. His thoughts are not our thoughts. But His ways are perfect and the plan He has for us is perfect. That is where we will ultimately be most content. I should have kept my focus on Him as I prayed for my desires. I should have added, *"but not my will, let Yours, be done,"* and then, just breathed.

Whatever you may be facing, surrender the situation and your desires to Him and allow God's will to be done. Give Him control. It does not matter if it is a job, marital issues, bankruptcy, or a miscarriage. The list can go on and on. When you release your will (what you want to happen) to God's will (what He is allowing to happen), He will give you strength, and a peace you never knew you could have as He lifts the boulder of heavy burden off your shoulder. Don't be afraid to ask His desire and plan for your situation, even if it's just an uneasy feeling. That does not mean your situation will magically disappear, but it does mean He will provide. He will walk you through it. He will give you a peace you cannot explain. He will lead you and give you direction for how to proceed. He will give you the strength to endure and you will become closer to Him and learn much because of it.

...weeping may last through the night,
but joy comes with the morning.

Psalm 30:5

Shattered

So do not be afraid, for I am with you.
Don't be discouraged, for I am your God.
I will strengthen you and help you;
I will uphold you with my victorious right hand.
Isaiah 41:10

March 29th—My first actual prenatal visit. I was really looking forward to it since I still had an uneasy feeling that I could not dismiss. I was going to ask her to do another ultrasound to be sure everything was progressing normally. And, it would be exciting to see the baby again. Being my first pregnancy, I was not sure when an ultrasound is usually done, or what the first pre-natal visit consisted of.

My appointment was at 9 am, but it might as well have been at 3 pm since time was dragging so slowly. I was very jittery and could not think of much else that morning. I sat down to read my devotional for the day—

Unto the Hills by Billy Graham. The scripture verse was Isaiah 41:10 (see above). The first paragraph read:

> ...Everyone who knows the Lord Jesus Christ can go through any problem, and face death, and still have the peace of God in his heart. When your spouse dies, or your children get sick, or you lose your job, you can have a peace that you don't understand. You may have tears at a graveside, but you can have an abiding peace, a quietness.

The devotional spoke about the availability of God's peace, at a moment's notice. But I felt there was more to it that I was not getting. Pacing back and forth in the living room, trying to understand what God wanted to say to me, I just couldn't sit still long enough to listen. I re-read it. Paced. Prayed. Nothing. But then again, I was more focused on the upcoming pre-natal visit than listening to the voice of God. So, I put the book down and left for the doctor.

Having nothing to compare it to, I assume the visit progressed as a standard prenatal visit. John stayed at work as this visit was predicted to be uneventful and we were not sure if she would do an ultrasound.

I don't recall at this point if I asked for the ultrasound or if it was protocol, but I got one. I was relieved that it was being done. The tech could not find the heartbeat. My heart began beating rather quickly. She said: "It's common at this early stage to not hear the heartbeat." I was fast to mention it was heard loud and clear at seven weeks. A few more clicks and taps with the keys and she decided to do a transvaginal ultrasound. Hmmm. More clicks and taps.

My heart was racing as she made an excuse to leave the room, then she came back in with the doctor, who repeated the process. I was almost to the point of panic, I knew something was not right...when she said it, "There is no heartbeat." I think I stopped breathing momentarily. *What???* She repeats, "There is no heartbeat," followed by some sort of possible explanation. All I remember hearing is the word, "non-viable." and "not going to carry to term."

Per her instructions, I sat up and got dressed. Then I went to meet her in her office. I listened to my options, "...let it abort naturally or go to the hospital for a D & C... either choice is acceptable...the hospital might be easier. Can I call anyone for you?"

"No. Can I use your phone?" (Keep in mind, at that time we did not have cell phones. They weren't as prevalent as they are today.) At that moment, working on autopilot and focusing on breathing was all I could do. I was trying not to cry—at least not yet.

I called John at work. "No heartbeat. Stopping at Gina's then going home. Yes. I'm fine." (No, *I am soooo far from fine. Breathe. Just breathe.*) Called Gina. "Hi. No heartbeat. See you in a few. No, I will drive..." I think my voice was barely a whisper. A few years later when we discussed this event, Gina revealed she did not recognize my voice on the phone; it took her a moment to realize who it was. She realized when she remembered I was going to my prenatal visit that day.

I find it interesting when you're walking in the early stages of your dreams being shattered, or just extreme life difficulties, how you never remember everything. You either remember nothing or you just remember snapshots. It truly is as if you're actually looking at a photograph of yourself at different times and different stages of a particular day. Memory snapshots. Maybe it's God's way of helping you deal with the situation because you don't need to remember everything. Maybe it's the brain's way of helping you run on autopilot, to do what you have to do. A coping mechanism.

About two years ago, a friend lost her husband suddenly. She does not know how she got through the day and made all the funeral arrangements. She remembers a few bits and pieces.

She remembers the friends who traveled with her to make the arrangements. Many, many people came to pay their respects, but she could not remember who. She ran on autopilot to do what needed to be done. Much of the rest is a blur. It does not matter who came—all that matters is they did.

I feel like I only remember snapshots of the remainder of that day; actually, the remainder of the weekend. As I was driving to Gina's, the flood gates opened, and I pulled over on the highway just before a Shell station. I was crying so hard I could not breathe, much less drive. I don't remember arriving at Gina's. I think I almost drove past her house to get to mine. Funny, I remember sitting on the highway just before the Shell gas station so clearly...the gray skies as it was going to rain...the pale blue sedan getting gas... Yet, I don't remember arriving at Gina's and only vaguely remember John getting there to drive me home. Snapshots.

The next thing I remember was waking from a nap, and realizing it was not a bad dream. I felt such a dark cloud of sadness. I sat up and swung my legs over the side of the bed, thinking, *This is really happening.* And the tears came... To this day John has never seen me cry so many tears. After trying for two and a half years, to have it end in a miscarriage was devastating. *Why? Wasn't this God's timing? We prayed. We waited. We served faithfully in various children's ministries. We gave Him the praise for answering our prayer for a child of our own...*

We drove back to Gina's in the late afternoon for dinner and a talk with our pastor. As we were driving, I remember telling John, "Child or no child, even if I don't understand, I will still serve Him faithfully." I had determined this in my heart, then professed it out loud. Looking back to that day, it is almost as if God had asked me, in the quietness of the car, "Will you still serve me, even without a child?"

Just a few short hours after my dreams of having a child were crushed, I professed out loud, "Yes, I will still serve Him." I find this to be an important lesson. When life hits you hard, there is an important decision to be made: Will you run to Him or from Him?

When our dreams are falling apart, in the midst of the hurt and pain, we are often not thinking rationally. It is easy to fall into a depression, deciding God has let us down or somehow failed us because we did not get what we wanted. Or we think He no longer loves us because He did not help us.

The heaviness that can come into your life with this kind of thinking is almost too much to bear. But isn't that what the enemy wants? John 10:10 reads, "The thief comes only in order to steal and kill and destroy" (AMP). The enemy of our souls waits for our weakest moments to plant seeds of doubt—to attack—and pull us away from God, the very One who can comfort us.

I love the second half of John 10:10 that reads, "I came that they may have and enjoy life, and have it in abundance [to the full, till it overflows]" (AMP). Enjoy life in the midst of shattered dreams? Yes. When you determine, dreams fulfilled or not, that you will continue to willingly and faithfully serve Him, He brings you comfort. He brings a peace you cannot explain; it's deep in your soul.

I am not saying you will be laughing a mile a minute. It is normal to go through a grieving process over our loss. But notice two words in that sentence: "go through." It's important we don't camp out there in the pain but continue to work through the process toward healing. He walks with us and helps us through it. As you go through, God brings strength and encouragement at the time you need it. This amazed me. Once I got past the initial hurt and loss, there was still a deep pain, a tender spot, but I found God still gave me strength right at the time I needed it. Not before. Not after. He was with me and helped me right then and there.

During my brief, eleven-and-a-half-week pregnancy, my focus was not on God. It was on the baby I so desperately wanted. Looking back, I don't think I wanted to know what He was saying that morning. Death and grieving were mentioned in that first paragraph of the devotional I was reading. That couldn't be me or my baby. And I was just too busy begging for the life of my child since the initial spotting incidence. It never occurred to me that regardless of what happened, God was in control, and His ways are perfect—like it or not.

Over the years I have learned that as I keep my focus on God, He will often provide me with insight or a Scripture verse, sometimes even a dream, just prior to a difficult situation. I may not know what situation I am about to face, but I have something to cling to and remind me He has it all under control.

On the morning my first prenatal visit, God tried to speak to me through that devotional, but I wasn't listening. I really wasn't focused on Him. I was just going through the motions until it was time to leave. Had I been paying attention, I may have been better prepared for what was ahead.

In the midst of difficult and painful circumstances, run to Him, knowing He has a reason for allowing this situation you are facing to come to pass. Keep your focus on Him and take time to listen. He will be faithful and give you strength.

In the end, you will find you are closer to Him and have a stronger faith than you ever thought possible. In the process, you may even minister to others going through similar situations. God always has a plan and a purpose. As we keep our focus on Him and allow His plan to unfold, He enables us to have peace even in the most difficult situations. This peace enables us to enjoy life in the midst of pain. And He will bring healing and strength to our lives.

DAWN M. MITCHELL

"The tragedy of life is not the fact of death...
but rather what dies inside us while we still live."
—Norman Cousins

DAWN M. MITCHELL

Answer from Unexpected Places

I raise my eyes toward the mountains.
Where will my help come from?
My help comes from the LORD,
the maker of heaven and earth.

Psalm 121: 1-2

My mom came to visit that weekend from Baltimore. She didn't know what to say to me. Really, no one did. But she was there. I still needed to decide how I wanted to handle the remainder of the pregnancy. *Do I let it go naturally? What should I expect? What kind of mental anguish will I have during the process? What if there is a complication? When will it happen or what if I am at work when it begins? Or do I just go to the hospital for a D&C?*

Honestly, I did not like either option. I wanted to carry a healthy baby to term. I walked around my small house looking at the few items I had begun collecting—

an antique full-size vintage Pram. (Looking back, the thing was beautiful, but a hand full as well, not easy to manipulate. But I had always wanted one and found a used one in excellent condition. Now the cats were sleeping in it.) A handmade baby cradle. A few hand-made baby sweaters picked up at yard sales with matching blankets and booties. A handmade blanket given to me as a gift from a patient at the office where I worked. She was one of the few I had told. *What was I going to do with all this stuff?* Our house was a small rancher without big storage areas, so hiding it from my daily view was going to be a bit difficult. I was thankful it was a few items and not a full-blown, already decorated nursery.

To some, wondering what I was going to do with a few items may sound trivial. But when you are walking in the early shattered state, you don't always think clearly. It's kind of like walking around in a daze, just going through the motions of day to day living. My health, emotionally and physically, was more important at that moment. And yet I was thinking about all these other things. Maybe just trying to not think about the pregnancy. I don't know.

I was not in any frame of mind to decide how to proceed. In reality, I did not want to make that decision. And no one would give me an opinion. It was the strangest thing, and I almost laugh at that now, because most of the time people love to give their opinion. You don't need to ask. My husband, my mom, Gina all said, "Both options are fine."

"It's up to you."

"I can't make that decision for you." And I was having difficulty making it for myself.

I was a bit frightened of either option. There were so many uncertainties with the natural route. Aside from the fact that I would know I was miscarrying at that time, there was the when, how long, severe cramping potential, and the risk of complications. The doctor had mentioned emergency D&C should a complication arise. But this would be natural, the way God intended, right?

Then there was the D&C route. At least I would be put to sleep and it would be all over when I woke up. Yet it is a surgical procedure, carrying increased risks. I associated a D&C with abortion. I know God had taken the soul of my child back home with Him, but still... *would this be considered abortion in God's eyes even though this was no longer a viable pregnancy?*

Our small rancher was in the mountains of Virginia, without any visible neighbors. We had beautiful views of nature regardless of the season. So, Saturday afternoon I walked out onto my deck. It was March 30th, it was a really warm, sunny day for it being the end of

March. My husband and mother were watching me like a hawk, not sure if or when I would crumble. I needed to breathe—a few minutes without being watched. There is just something about looking towards the sun and feeling the warmth on your face. So, I stood there on the deck looking at the trees, feeling the warmth of the sun, and asked God, "What am I to do? Please, I need some direction."

"Please listen and answer me, for I am overwhelmed by my troubles" (Psalm 55:2).

A few moments later, John brought me the phone.

My father-in-law had called. He and my mother-in-law were both aware of the situation. I was blessed with wonderful in-laws and my father-in-law was not one to tip toe around the tulips when he had something to say. Throughout the conversation, he voiced his opinion. When I say he voiced his opinion, I mean he offered his opinion without my asking for it. It was the opinion I so desperately needed to hear.

His opinion was that I should have the doctor do the D&C at the hospital, because then it would all be over. No guessing. No potential complications. It would all be okay. Our conversation was very brief. At that moment, in the warmth of the sun, I felt I had my answer. I had a decision and would follow through with the D&C.

There was a check in my spirit that I knew it was how I should proceed.

I stood there, enjoying the fresh air for a few more minutes, tears streaming down my cheeks...and finally called the doctor with my decision. She was going to call when everything was scheduled with the hospital and give me all the details.

I always found it interesting that God used my father-in-law to bring me an answer that day. He and I had a rough start to our relationship. He did not "adore" me like a father-in-law might adore their daughter-in-law. But we treated each other with respect and, as time went on, we got along well. I could not ask for more than that.

Yet he was the one willing to voice his opinion. And I needed to hear it. I needed someone to take the reins and help me. In reality, I think I wanted the hospital route, but wanted someone to tell me that was is okay to do so. Once he said, "It's okay. Then it will all be over with," I felt the matter was settled and I had peace deep within my soul. I had a check in my spirit, that I knew it was okay. I was so grateful for his candidness, and I have never forgotten it.

It is amazing how God can provide our answer from the most unexpected place. We need to be open to how He chooses to bring our answer, and from whom He chooses to bring it. When you are distraught and walking through the initial state of hurt and pain, I am not saying you should follow the opinion of every person who offers it, or even the first person, I am saying to ask God for direction and be open to receive that direction from whatever source He decides to provide it. Read His Word and think on any Scripture He allows to leap off the page at you. Or if you are seeking guidance and an opinion is offered, there will be a check within your spirit, "You know that you know," along with a deep peace directing you, "This is how to proceed."

Grabbing the first thing that sounds good, yet may not be His will, just to have an answer and proceed, may make you even more confused and distraught. I have noticed sometimes people in difficult situations will choose what seems easier and less work because they just want it to be over, rather than waiting and doing what they should do, and it only lands them into further difficulties. Easier does not always equal better.

I will call to you whenever I'm in trouble,
and you will answer me.
Psalm 86:7

DAWN M. MITCHELL

Lazarus

He shouted with a loud voice,
"Lazarus, come out!"
Out came the man who had been dead.
John 11:43-44

A weight had been lifted off my shoulders once this decision had been made. I know that sounds crazy. It was a check mark on the invisible list of items to be completed for it to all be over. The doctor had called back, and I was to be at the hospital at 8am on Monday. The fact that I was not going to carry to term was beginning to settle in. All my hopes and dreams for this child had vanished. Psalm 56:8 reads, "You keep track of all my sorrows. You have collected all my tears in your bottle. You have recorded each one in your book." I knew He was aware of the depth of my pain and I hoped He had a really big bottle.

I don't remember much of the remainder of the day. Napping. Daydreaming about what could have been.

Once the decision had been made on how to handle the remainder of the pregnancy, it was easy to let my mind wander. I thought about the wonderful father my husband would have been. It always amazed me how well he did with children, how patient he was. He enjoyed showing them things that would make their eyes go huge with surprise. And kids seemed to love him. And yet, at this time our child was not meant to be.

Sunday, we went to church. It was a probably considered a small church by today's standards. The people who attended were close knit and had big faith. It was a very loving and caring church with a wonderful pastor. It was our week to teach children's church and I was so thankful someone else was covering the class for us. I have no idea what the pastor spoke about. I was there physically and that is where it ended.

All I could think about was Jesus calling Lazarus out of the grave. I pictured it in my mind over and over again. Jesus saying, "Lazarus, come out!" And out he came. Just like that. Martha was quick to point out that he had been in the grave for four days and the smell would be awful. But she knew God would give Jesus whatever he asked. (See John 11: 22.) She believed. And Lazarus walked right out, grave clothes and all. Good as new. "Didn't I tell you that you would see God's glory if you believe?" (John 11:40)

We went back to church for the Sunday night service. I always loved those services. They were so different from the morning services. There seemed to be a freedom during the Sunday night services that was not there in the morning. There was more of a freedom to follow where the Spirit led. Now don't get me wrong, our pastor always followed the promptings of the Holy Spirit, regardless of the service. It just always seemed to me that those who returned for the Sunday night service were really hungry for a move of God and were open to whatever He chose to do. When you combine hungry people, who come to worship with no concern about the limits of time there is an openness for God to do as He pleases.

After the worship and before the message, Pastor felt lead to pray for those who had needs. Those who needed a physical healing could come up to the altar and be anointed with oil and be prayed for. Our church had some serious prayer warriors who also went up to pray. Several people went up for prayer, including myself.

When Pastor got to me, he asked me my request. I told him, "If Jesus could raise Lazarus from the grave after four days, then raising this baby that is still in the womb and allowing me to carry to term and have this child is nothing." And I believed it. Tears streaming down my face, my words were barely a whisper. Until that moment, only a few knew that the pregnancy had become non-viable. Now they all knew.

"Hear me as I pray, O Lord. Be merciful and answer me" (Psalm 27:7).

I closed my eyes and lifted my hands in praise to God as Pastor began to pray. I believed with everything in me that God could do it. I was going to have the hospital do another ultrasound before the procedure because I was believing God for a miracle. Maybe that was why He had allowed this to happen—He wanted others to see a miracle.

As Pastor finished praying and I wiped the tears from my face, I heard God audibly say, "No, this is not meant to be." I heard Him as if He were standing right in front of me. This is one of the few times I can actually say I audibly heard God speak to me. I knew, beyond a shadow of a doubt, my answer was no. He was not going to breathe life back into my child. I returned to my seat. Numb. I was numb for the remainder of the service. There was no need to repeat the ultrasound. The answer was, "No." I knew for certain, and I had peace. God showed me mercy after hearing the prayer of His daughter who desperately wanted a child, and He answered quickly. And I heard Him loud and clear.

There are no words to express how grateful to God I was at that moment. In my despair, He showed me great kindness and mercy in answering my request immediately and so clearly. He did not allow me to wonder and hope and believe for something He had determined was not going to happen. It was not His will.

Even when God says, "No," we need to be thankful. Thankful that He is allowing His will and desires to be fulfilled in our lives. Thankful for His timely answers. If we really want God's will in our lives, then we should be equally happy regardless of whether the answer is "yes" or "no." We should rejoice for the "yes" and rejoice for the "no." Think about it... Even during the most painful times in our lives, He only wants what is best for us and has allowed the situation to happen for a reason. A reason we may, or may not, ever become aware of. And who knows what He is saving or protecting us from when He does say, "no." I wish I had learned this lesson sooner.

Monday morning, we were off to the hospital. It was April 1st. April Fool's Day. Hah! When was I going to wake up from this bad dream? Once we arrived at the hospital, no one knew where we were to go. It was creepy. I remember saying to John and my mom: "I hope this isn't one of those things where you go in for a simple procedure and come out missing an arm." They did not find this amusing as that had happened somewhere just a week or so prior due to mixed up hospital charts. We all felt better when we stumbled into my doctor.

She got me settled into a room until my procedure. I was still so certain of my answer from God I did not have her repeat the ultrasound. We declined to do genetic testing even though my father-in-law offered to cover the expense. We assumed since we finally conceived, that it would easily happen again.

Once everything was finished and I was out of recovery, we went home. I had the remainder of the week off work. Mom left to head back to Baltimore to go back to work herself. And time marched on...

Dear Lord,

I would have loved to have held my daughter on my lap and tell her about You.

But since I did not get the chance, would You please hold her on Your lap and tell her about me?

—Dawn

DAWN M. MITCHELL

Wholly Follow the Lord

Let your unfailing love surround us, Lord—
for our hope is in you.
Psalm 33:22

I went back to work the following week and life went back to normal; as normal as it could be at that point. I was sad and disappointed, but work kept me occupied for the most part. We waited a few months to let my body head and my mind regroup before we began trying to conceive again. We assumed since I had conceived once, my body now knew what to do and the second time would be much easier.

It did not happen that way. The months turned into a year. We did everything we could on our end. We prayed. We kept track of my temperature to watch for ovulation. (Your body temperature increases a few degrees when you ovulate.) It is an easy way of determining optimal fertile days. It was not ideal for good lovemaking between a husband and wife. It takes the joy of sexual intimacy that God created between a husband and a wife and puts the focus on having a baby and adds much stress. The joy was gone—it was all about conceiving.

At the time, there were a few articles coming on infertility. The high cost of infertility is not just financial but takes a toll on couples in general. We read almost anything we could find. There was very little information twenty-one years ago when we were going through it. One article we found especially well written covered the various costs of infertility treatment because insurance companies did not provide coverage then like they do now. But it also discussed the toll it took on couples. Many ended up in divorce and for various reasons. Some because the stress of infertility itself pulled them apart. And if that didn't, the financial strain did. A few divorced because they did not agree to a life without children and left their spouse for someone who could give them what they desired.

The article was an eye opener for us because we could fully understand how it takes a toll on couples. God in His mercy and wisdom used this article to help John and I talk through these issues. He said, "I married you because I love you, not because you could have children. I want you more than I want children." (Have I mentioned yet that I have the best husband ever?) To this day, I still remember the moment he said those words. They were powerful to me.

We also agreed ahead of time that we would not let infertility, or the financial strain of it, affect our marriage. Should we consider infertility treatment, we would prayerfully consider options then proceed as our finances allowed. At that point, we had not yet seen an infertility specialist or began any infertility treatment. We were just reading up on it, uncertain if we should really look into it. We just could not decide if we would be taking the matter into our own hands and out of God's if we had infertility assistance. So, we waited and continued to pray to know His will.

For me to not be able to have a child made me feel like less of a woman. Like I was not good enough, like there was something wrong with me. I remember being very angry at my body because it would not work right. I felt isolated. I did not know anyone having the same issues. It seemed rather uncommon. And unfair. I prayed for strength and help in dealing with my emotions. At the time, I did not know how to release them to God. I thought I was, but in reality, I was just pushing them down. Stuffing them way down.

I remember chatting with a woman after the evening service one Sunday. She had been praying for John and I to have a child for several months. She told me she finally asked God, "Lord, when will you answer my prayer?" And she felt like the Lord responded, "This time next year she will have twins, a boy and a girl." She was so excited she had to share it with me. It made me feel so hopeful and excited myself. *Could it really be so?* I had written it in my prayer journal in case it did come to pass. But I also thought it best to pray over it and asked God to confirm it through someone else if it was true. I never received that confirmation and nine months later I was still not pregnant.

Driving home late one night I remember hearing a song on the radio. The song was entitled, "Jesus has a Rocking Chair" by the Greenes. It was about the loss of a child and how "Jesus has a rocking chair." I could just picture Jesus sitting in a rocking chair, rocking my baby. I just bawled the remainder of the trip home, thinking about my child being rocked by Jesus. I tried to tell Gina about it. I have no idea if she understood a word I said or not. Although it does amaze me how well she has learned to understand me through my tears. She thought I should name the baby. She said it can often help provide closure. I loved the idea. We prayed about it and since I had secretly hoped for a little girl, we decided to name the baby Anna Rose. We combined the first name of John's grandmother and the first name of my great-grandmother.

The desire to have a child seemed to consume my thoughts. I prayed about it almost, if not daily, asking God to grant us this blessing. He was the creator of life, and my hope was in Him to answer my prayer. John and I were still serving in children's ministries, and yet we did not have children of our own. Honestly, sadness and disappointment occasionally came to visit. A lot actually. Yet we tried to trust God for His provision.

God did not seem to be answering for us, but He was answering it for everyone else. Everywhere we looked people were having, or had, babies. A few years had passed when my brother called with the "happy" news that he and his wife were expecting their first child. While I was really happy for them, it took everything within me to not cry while I was on the phone with him.

Then there was listening to my mother talk about "the baby." Her first grandchild. My grandmother's first great-grandchild. "The baby." My daughter should have been the first grandchild. The range of emotions that seared through me at this point were very difficult to manage. Now I had the "excitement" of watching someone very close to me have their first child and live all the dreams I had not gotten to live. My dreams... Just as I thought it was beginning to get a little bit easier.

My mom would update me on "the baby." She and Granny went shopping and bought things for "the baby." She shared with me the dreams she had for "the baby" and what wonderful parents my brother and his wife would be. (And they have been fantastic parents.) "The baby." All I could do was clench my jaws together to not cry, and to listen. I was interested. I was happy for them. After all, this was my brother. But I was also so... jealous... hurt... angry... need I go on?

When your dreams have been crushed, eventually, it does get easier. But when you are faced with watching someone close to you receive the blessing you not only lost, but had been desperately seeking, it can be a bit difficult. I was not prepared for it. I wish I had been. By this point I was not talking about my situation with anyone, except my husband and Gina sometimes. I tried not to discuss it at all. I was embarrassed to let anyone know how I really felt. I was happy for my family but the envy, anger, and embarrassment I felt far surpassed any happiness.

I was focusing more and more on my broken dreams. My daughter was in the rocking chair with Jesus and not here with me. Several years had passed, so being hopeful was becoming more difficult, especially now.

God gently brought the question to my attention, "But isn't that what Satan wants?" Yes. Yes, it is. The only way he can really get to us is through our thoughts. To get us focused on what we lost, or don't have, or can't do. He tells us it will never happen, causing us to lose our hope and faith in the One who really has our best interest in mind. This leads us to a life of defeat, never accomplishing what God wants us to do.

God graciously reminded me— "Greater is He that is in me that he that is in the world" (1 John 4:4). Let me say that again...

"Greater is He that is in you than He that is in the world."

With His help and strength, you will get through this difficult time. He will be with you. Sometimes in the midst of our hurt and pain we forget that we are not alone. He is always there.

I remember asking God: "What can I do for you? How can I use these trials to bring You glory? I don't understand why You have chosen for us to go through this. How do I accept these trials with joy? Please, God, change my heart and my attitude." His response to me was, "wholeheartedly follow the Lord" (Joshua 14:8).

He wants us to follow Him with our entire heart; to keep our focus on Him and not the situation. Taking the focus off ourselves and keeping it on Him opens us up to be a blessing to others; possibly to people going through situations similar to our own. And it allows us to walk in the peace and calmness He provides. It helps us to let go of our situation and give it to Him.

2 Corinthians 1:4 says, "He comforts us in all our troubles so that we can comfort others. When they are troubled, we will be able to give them the same comfort God has given us" (NLT),

God provided me strength and calmness when I talked with my family about "the baby." Looking back, it amazes me how God helped me at the time I needed it. Not before, not after, but right on time as I kept my focus on Him and tried to use my life, even with my shattered dreams and pain, to bring Him glory and be happy for someone else receiving what I had so desperately desired.

The baby shower was at my Grandmother's house. God gave me the ability to go and be there without crying. I may have cried when I got back to Virginia. But I made it through the shower, and I was thankful for that, thankful I could be there for my sister-in-law. But deep down, I felt there was bitterness brewing. Emotions I had not dealt with were beginning to bubble to the surface. I just kept stuffing them back down.

Building Walls

"When under attack, when facing new challenges,
In all seasons, in all times,
Call on the name of the Lord, & He will help you."
—Jim Cymbala
Fresh Wind, Fresh Fire

Shortly after my sister-in-law's baby shower I received the "happy" news from Gina that she was pregnant. It took her four months to tell me. We had been unsuccessful for so many years at this point, I can only imagine how painful it must have been for her to finally tell me. This blessing was a surprise. Through the process of telling me about it, she revealed she had an uneasy feeling about the pregnancy.

She had two wonderful teenage boys, so this was to be her third. God had given me the opportunity to comfort her and pray for her and her baby. I am amazed at how He gave me strength to pray and words of encouragement for her—right at the time I needed it.

Afterward, I felt a bit blindsided. She was four months pregnant, but she had concealed it well. I felt I just lost one of the two people I could talk to. If it were even possible, my feelings of isolation grew. It seemed every woman I came in contact with was pregnant or had just had a baby. I continued to pray for strength in dealing with my own infertility and everyone else being pregnant. It was becoming increasingly difficult to deal with and not asking God, "Why not me? I'm here. I'm ready. What is wrong with me?"

Why wouldn't God work out a baby and all the details in our lives when we had clearly been waiting so long? He was giving them out right and left to everyone else, even to those who did not ask. What about us? It was very painful. But I kept trusting God had a plan for our lives and I wanted His plan to unfold above all else, including my desires. And I knew that His grace would always be enough to see me through. Anytime I silently called on Him to give me strength, He was right there to provide. But I just didn't understand.

As time went on, I really struggled with my emotions. I was feeling frustrated, hurt, bitter, angry. It was difficult seeing others pregnant and even my best friend being given a blessing from above she did not ask for. I felt as if I was constantly asking God for His forgiveness for my wayward emotions.

God was always faithful to provide me with encouragement from His Word. "Trust in Him at all times, you people. Pour out your heart before Him, God is a refuge for us" (Psalm 62:8).

Gina was such a blessing to me during her pregnancy. She shared as much of it with me as I could handle. I traveled with her to some doctor appointments, ultrasounds... It was interesting to see how it could have been if my pregnancy had progressed to full term. It was always difficult hearing the heartbeat. I was amazed at the wonder of God, yet sad for my own pregnancy that had ended too soon.

My life has been so blessed by Gina's friendship. We have shared so much of our lives together. There just are not words to describe. She allowed me to share her experiences and wasn't offended if I cried. She invited me into the delivery room with her and her husband to see the birth of her third son. I opted not to as I felt it was more of a private moment between a husband and wife as their child entered the world. But I was there with a Winnie the Pooh shortly after he arrived.

Sometimes I would look at her and feel so envious. She had two wonderful boys and now a third, beautiful baby. She was able to stay at home and raise them. My sister-in-law also eventually left her job to stay home and raise her daughter. I just cannot fathom that life.

As time went on, envy was added to the list of emotions I had to manage. I was happy for Gina and my brother and his wife; but hurt for myself. Up to this point, I felt I had been doing well. I sought God. I asked Him to somehow be glorified through my life in this situation. He was using me to bring comfort or pray for other women in similar situations. He was putting women in my life who needed prayer due to concerns about their own pregnancies, recent miscarriages, or infertility. God gave me the strength and grace for each of these situations, and I was so thankful, thinking something good would come out of it; and yet I still struggled.

I knew this was part of God's desire for us at this time in our lives. His plans for me are different than the plans He has for others. His plans for each of us are unique. At the time, I was asking for a child of our own and strength in managing my wayward emotions. But not once did I stop and ask, "What are your plans for me?" I wanted my life to glorify Him as I went through this trial, but I didn't seek *His* plans for my life.

One night we got a phone call from another close relative. His wife was pregnant. He was happy, she was not. She was crying her eyes out as she had wanted to wait a bit longer before having a child since they had not been married very long. Talk about a hard pill to swallow. This one almost choked me to death. I cried a river of tears. This took me almost to my limit. After trying unsuccessfully for over five years and crying almost every month because it did not happen, I could not fathom someone not being excited to have a child. And I did not want to understand.

So here I am, having had a miscarriage just days before my second trimester—praying month after month, year after year—with nothing. Then I have a sister-in-law with a beautiful little girl, received because they were trying. My best friend with the sweetest little boy, just because God wanted to bless her, and a third family member who is pregnant but not ready. Three different situations, three babies. And my dreams still lay in broken pieces.

The wayward emotions I thought I was dealing with so well came bubbling up to the surface. So, what did I do? I continued to ask God for His help as I tried to stuff down all those emotions; trying to pretend they weren't there. Pretending I was not upset, or angry, or jealous. To some degree, I think I felt as if I was not allowed to have those emotions; I should be happy for every pregnant woman and want to know every detail of their pregnancy. The persistent emotions were part of the grieving process and I kept pushing them down rather than deal with them.

I was so hurt. And confused. So, I "walled up." I already felt very isolated, and I built my wall a bit higher. Very few were let in. Very few. I was fragile. I needed protection. Not only do walls prevent others from coming in, but they prevent you from coming out. It's a false sense of protection.

But notice I say, "hurt" instead of "broken." My downfall at this point was that I "built a wall," and in doing so I did not allow myself to become broken. Oh, I was broken all right. But not broken open in a way that allows God to mend and heal and restore joy and life.

Instead of allowing the situation to take me to my knees, I built a wall. God had to spend years—and I do mean years—taking down that wall, layer by layer. I still prayed and sought Him, but penetrating a wall is difficult. Walls are strong, built to stand their ground, to protect. Walls bring isolation. I felt even more like a failure.

Looking back, I wish I would have let it break me, take me to my knees. I wish I would have taken a step back and asked God, "What are your plans for me? What do You wish to accomplish through this?" God could have done so much more in me and through me. I would not have wasted so many years of my life struggling with negative emotions and keeping people (pregnant women and young children especially) at arm's length.

It is very difficult when your dreams are shattered, and you see everyone else living them. When you feel you are at your limit—your breaking point—allow it to take you to your knees and surrender the situation to God. Seek His will and purpose. He does have a reason and a purpose.

At that time, I had not surrendered it to God. I still had not said, "Okay Lord, let YOUR will be done. I give up. Please take away all this hurt and sadness." To become broken is to allow yourself to become moldable clay in the hands of the Potter, allowing His will to come to pass. Walls are a form of *self*-protection. They don't bend or give. They are not pliable. They don't grow; and can't be stretched. Often, we grow and learn the most about ourselves and God when we allow ourselves to become broken, pliable in the hands of the One who created us; the One who has a perfect plan for each of us. I spent so many years carrying around hurt, envy, and longing for a child—and I did not have to. And you don't either, regardless of the shattered dream you are facing.

I am thankful that God never gave up on me. I am thankful He continued to pursue me. He was willing to peel apart each layer to bring healing and restore my joy. He will do the same for you too, if you are willing to surrender your broken pieces to Him and seek His will and desire for your life.

DAWN M. MITCHELL

He heals the broken hearted and binds up their wounds.
His understanding is infinite.
Psalm 147:3,5

DAWN M. MITCHELL

Emotions

Think of various tests you encounter as occasions for joy.
After all, you know that the testing of your faith produces
endurance. Let this endurance complete its work so that you
may be fully mature, lacking nothing.
James 1: 2-4 (CEB)

So maybe at this point you're thinking, *Okay lady, get a grip. So you couldn't have a child. It could be so much worse.* And you are right. It could be worse. I am thankful to God it isn't. It took me years to realize that. We all have dreams and aspirations. As children, we are raised with the thought of growing up, going to college, getting a good job, getting married, buying a house, and having children—it's just life. (I won't even dive into all this being followed by becoming a grandparent.) I have seen the joy children bring their parents. When a little boy comes running to his momma after church when she goes to collect him from nursery. Or when a little girl goes running up, arms outstretched, to her dad. I see it.

I've seen the heartache too. But I don't ever think I have heard a parent speak regret over having their children.

Many people live with shattered dreams. Bad things happen. I've never really been one to ask God, "Why me?" The way I see it, *Why not me?* Why not any of us? He is God and we are to believe and trust Him regardless of our circumstances. Now, as I go through difficult situations, I try to seek His guidance and ask, "Is there something you are trying to teach me, something that I should learn through this situation?" And, "How do you want me to proceed? How can I bring you glory through this?" Life is much easier when I keep my focus on Him, instead of the situation.

When our dreams lay in pieces on the ground, whether it's a job loss, death of a spouse, bankruptcy, miscarriage, there are five stages of emotions we work through. The first is shock or denial. You just can't believe this has happened and you feel like you are in a daze; just going through the motions. You don't know what to say, what to think. You wonder if and when will you wake up from this dream.

When I initially found out I was not going to carry to term, I left the doctor's office and drove to Gina's in a daze, remembering nothing but the gas station until I woke up from a nap. Then I began crying because it was not a dream.

Second is grief. You may cry at times and it can hit you at odd moments, triggered unexpectedly. I found, once I got through this stage, that occasionally something would hit me just right and the tears would come, briefly. And it could be months or years later.

Third is anger. Anger over the situation. Or "Why me? Why did this happen?" I struggled with anger because I didn't know how or where, or to whom, to direct my anger. I didn't feel like I should be angry at God. He is God, who am I to question Him?

I was angry at myself. Angry at my body that it wouldn't work right. Angry that I didn't carry to term and was having difficulty conceiving again. It took two and a half years the first time. I thought this time would be easier. I was angry I didn't have the genetic testing done on the baby when I was at the hospital for the D&C. At least this would have provided more information on my baby and the pregnancy. *Was the baby a boy or a girl?* I hated Mother's Day. I was envious and angry over those who were able to conceive. The list of things I was angry about could go on and on.

Still, I kept praying and seeking God. Seeking His forgiveness. Wondering if it was my fault. *Was there some sort of sin in my life that cause this to happen? Was it the car accident and the seatbelt pulling too tight? Or did God just choose to take her home?* I didn't want to be angry at

God. His ways are perfect. His choices for us are perfect. How could I be angry at Him?

I dealt with this stage a few years. Years. And it was painful. I didn't want to admit I was angry at all, especially at God, for allowing it to happen. Driving in my SUV one day, praying, He impressed upon my heart that it's okay to be angry, it's what I do with the anger that matters. I can still see myself on a sunny day on a back-mountain road, stunned because God said it's okay to be angry. But I also realized at that moment I was angry at Him for taking her home and I didn't want to be. I asked Him to help me, to forgive me. I didn't want to be angry at all, especially at Him. I was crying and actually yelled out loud at God, then told Him He *"has to help me!"* (After yelling at God in my car I wondered if He thought, *Okay. You get one of those blaming Me, yelling at Me moments.*)

Sunday was Mother's Day. Pastor preached on the "heart of a mother." I wanted to leave. To get up and march my feet right out of that sanctuary. I had no business being there. I was not a mother and did not need to hear another sermon on how wonderful it is to be a mother, and how warm and fuzzy her heart is... *blah, blah, blah...*

Yes, bitterness is attached to envy and can rear its ugly head if you're not careful. Since leaving was not an option and I truly desired more of God, I asked Him what I was to get from the service. (Believe me when I say I am not perfect. Yes, I asked God to show me, but I wasn't completely sincere as I couldn't fathom what I could get out of another Mother's Day service. In His kindness, He showed me.) A few moments later, the tone of the service changed to the reality that Mother's Day is not happy for everyone, some feel hurt or sadness. And the tears came. As I went up to the altar afterwards to pray, I really sought God for release of all these feelings that I knew were not of Him—anger, bitterness, envy. I just could not seem to let go. And God, in His mercy, spoke to my heart, to write it all in a letter—to pour out my heart to Him. The letter was to represent all my hurt, anger, bitterness, etc., and I was to leave it on the altar that night. It seemed crazy at first but made sense. It would be a visible representation of my emotions.

I did just that. I poured my heart out onto those now tear-stained pages. I left nothing out. I addressed it to God. We arrived at church early that night and I went to the altar, prayed over the letter, and left it there in its sealed envelope. Pastor mentioned to me that I left something at the altar. I explained I could not pick it up but asked him if he would pick it up and pray over it, and then rip it up.

God gave me a tangible way to leave my anger and hurt at the altar, and I walked away feeling like I could breathe again. I wanted so much for Him to be glorified through my life and my situation. If I have to go through it God, be glorified. I was worried my wayward, uncontrolled emotions were preventing that. He provided a way out. He will always provide a way out. (See 1 Corinthians 10:13.)

The fourth stage is depression. Things may seem pointless and you just feel like being left alone. This is a normal part of the grieving process, but you don't want it to persist too long. Don't allow yourself to camp out here indefinitely.

The final stage is acceptance. You begin to realize you will get through this. God has not left you. You wake up one morning and realize the sun is still shinning and you feel hope.

It's important to work through these stages, seeking God, for healing and restoration. The goal is to move through the various stages, not camp out longer than necessary at any one stage.

Along with asking God for the blessing of a child, I was seeking His help with all the emotions I felt. I really wanted to move past them. I didn't want bitterness and envy to stay in my heart. I've seen how it can rot people from the inside out.

I also want to mention that God does not allowed difficult situations to happen because He is angry with you or because you have done something wrong. When you come to Him, sincerely seeking His forgiveness, He is faithful and forgives. He will not hold a grudge and bring about punishment later. He loves you immeasurably. We cannot fathom the depth of love He has for us. He has our best interest in mind when He allows our dreams to be crushed. Even when we don't understand, He does, and has it all under control. He wants only what is best for us.

Losing one thing may be bring about something better later. Sometimes, "No" is the best answer for us. We need to be willing to hear His answer, even when it is not the answer we desire.

Those who stand firm during testing are blessed. They are tried and true. They will receive the life God has promised to those who love him as their reward.

James 1:12 (CEB)

Council of God

There are many plans in a man's heart, nevertheless the counsel of the Lord, that shall stand.
Proverbs 19:21

I think it's very important for us to look to God and not man for counsel, just at His Word says. God brought this point to my attention at a women's retreat in September 2000.

Every fall, the women of our district church had an overnight women's retreat. Usually, several ladies from my church attended. These events were so much fun, and we all looked forward to going each year. On Friday, there was a morning service, workshops on various topics to choose from during late morning and early afternoon, and an evening service. Saturday morning had one service. Women could attend any part or all the events.

Aside from the fellowship with each other, we really looked forward to the Friday night services. The messages were usually amazing. Almost everyone came with an expectancy for a move of God, a willingness to linger and wait for Him.

On this particular Friday night, as in the past, you could really feel God's presence in the room. Unfortunately, I don't remember the speaker's name, but she talked about God's timing. We may not know why God does what He does, answers, or delays answering prayer, healing, etc. We need to trust God and His perfect plan. He has His reasons and timing for things.

God used her testimony in an amazing way that night. She'd had menstrual problems for nine years and was prayed for and anointed with oil, but still had issues.

After an emergency hysterectomy, the anesthesiologist came into her room to find out who she was. He explained, after he put her to sleep, she spoke for four hours in his native language, telling him of his life. They talked for a bit. That night he became a believer and got his life right with God. God used her and spoke through her. God let her know at that moment that she had suffered for nine years for his soul!

This is the type of story that just leaves you in awe. God is so amazing. God used her in such a unique way to touch another person's life, leading to his salvation. Her suffering had a purpose.

At the end of the service, during the altar call, I debated about going up for prayer. I had been so many times, and God had helped me with so much of the hurt and pain. But could my pain make a difference in the life of someone else? I just stood there, in front of my seat, debating and worshiping God.

Finally, a close friend who was next to me, leaned over to tell me that for the last fifteen minutes she had felt I needed to go up for prayer, so I finally did. While I was waiting, I enjoyed the worship music and presence of God. When the speaker got to me to pray for me, she said, "You know what they say, 'Adopt and you'll have one of your own!'" We prayed and talked a little more, but the moment she said that, I felt a change in my spirit.

I questioned if this was from God and decided to pray about it. It seemed like such a strange thing to say. I mentioned it to my friend that night and she said she would pray too. I could not understand why I was to go up for prayer for that.

One thing that came to mind Sunday morning during my time with God was, *At least I didn't take it as God's immediate answer-but questioned and prayed if this was truly God and His will.* During the worship service that morning, my friend was still wondering why too. It came to her mind to, "Look to God and not man. Trust Him."

As I was reading my Bible that following Tuesday, I came across the commentary for Proverbs 24:6 ("An honest answer is like a kiss on the lips.") and it said, "Sometimes even the godliest person can unknowingly give us the wrong advice."

"Sometimes even the godliest person can unknowingly give us the wrong advice." I felt I had confirmation that her comment to me that Friday night was not from God. She was a godly woman with an amazing testimony. I am absolutely certain she meant no harm, but it caused me to question.

You see, what I have not shared with you yet, is that my husband and I prayed and fasted about having children of our own, and if God's plan was for us to adopt a child. After much time in prayer, we both felt the answer was, "No." We were not to adopt. We were beginning to realize God's plan for us may be to not have children at all, but we had not given up hope. Who knew if God would be gracious to us and grant us the child we so desired? But we were confident adoption was not His plan for us.

So, when she told me to, "Adopt and I will have one of my own," it made me question if we were on the correct path. Did we misunderstand God? Was adoption His plan for us and we had wasted time? It was also an insensitive comment, one many have made trying to be helpful and make light of a painful situation. All I could think was, I went up there for that?

Questioning is good because it causes you to seek answers, for confirmation. Where you seek those answers is of utmost importance.

It's okay to discuss your situation with a godly friend. When seeking counsel, it must come from a godly source. Proverbs 25:19 reads: "Confidence in an unfaithful man in time of trouble is like a bad tooth and a foot out of joint." Ouch!

Often, our godly friends can pray with us or for us, offer insight and encouragement, and sometimes be brutally honest in a way that steps on our toes. Sometimes we do need our toes stepped on to get us back in line with things and it's safer when it comes from a close friend, because we know it is based in love.

Keep in mind, there may be a check in your spirit if something is, or is not, in line with where God is leading you. If something feels off, question God. Search His Word. Don't assume.

The final say should always come from God and His Word. He can provide us wisdom and counsel in so many ways—through His Word, through our godly friends, through our circumstances. "God causes everything to work together for those the good of those who love God" (Romans 8:28).

I am thankful God has taught me to bring everything to Him, to question and seek His counsel above all else.

If you don't know what you're doing, pray to the Father.
He loves to help. You'll get his help, and won't be
condescended to when you ask for it.
Ask boldly, believingly without a second thought.
James 1:5-6 (MSG)

Drowning

"If I could wish for my life to be perfect, it would be tempting, but I would have to decline, for life would no longer teach me anything."
-Allyson Jones, English Physician

Sometimes we do wish for our lives to be perfect, or different, or just...easy. Yet, we learn so much through the trials and difficult circumstances in our lives. They challenge us, enable us to become stronger, and cause us to become closer to God.

August of 2010 began a year of challenges that impacted not just John and I, but my mother and brother as well (especially my mother) and changed our lives.

That August, my mother, Mary, was taken to the hospital via ambulance. She was not very coherent and couldn't walk. She was hospitalized for about a week. I kept missing the doctors when they visited, so I was not sure what the problem was. She didn't seem to remember, and the nurses were not allowed to reveal a diagnosis; it had to come from the doctor. I left messages for the doctor to call me. He never did. Upon her release, one of the nurses finally told me she was in liver failure. She said the specialist that came to see her said, "She is in liver failure, call me when she gets insurance." And home she went.

I was furious that the doctor didn't even have the courtesy to call me. I had Medical Power of Attorney paperwork and her permission, so he could speak with me. This was important because in liver failure, toxins build up in your body and your body can't properly function. These toxins also affect your mind, how you think and remember things. My mom couldn't remember anything, so she wasn't able to tell me what the doctors had said. It was kind of the nurse to tell me.

I didn't know what to do, where to go, or how to proceed. But God is amazing and His timing, as always, is perfect. A few days later, at work, one of my patients just happened to be a hepatologist—a liver specialist from Johns Hopkins Hospital. So, I gently started to pick his brain. My mother's prior hepatologist had retired, so I was hoping he would at least tell me how to proceed. Once he realized I was asking about my mom, he began asking very specific questions. Dr. G. had her in his office that week and took her on as his patient!

So, how did we get to this point? In the early 1970s my mom had emergency surgery because her had gall-bladder ruptured. My brother and I were maybe seven and eight years old at the time, if that. I still remember my grandmother and aunt coming over in the middle of the night and my mom leaving in an ambulance. That tends to stick with a kid, when their only parent leaves in an ambulance. During the surgery she needed a blood transfusion. The blood she received during surgery carried hepatitis. (At that time, blood was not screened and tested as thoroughly as it is now.)

A few weeks or so after surgery she was told she had viral hepatitis from the blood she received during the transfusion, but she would live a long and healthy life. Thirty years later she was diagnosed with severe liver cirrhosis, so she was under the care of a hepatologist and managing very well. Then he retired. In addition, she lost her job of twenty-some years, and her health benefits. And here we were, few years later, with liver failure and no health insurance.

Dr. G. called me at home to give me the run down on Mom. She was in liver failure and without a transplant, she had possibly a year to live. He advised me to go over to her house that night to fill out information for health insurance and medical assistance so it could be mailed in the morning—there was no time to waste.

He explained how the toxins building up from a mal-functioning liver would affect her comprehension and he wasn't sure what she was, or was not, fully under-standing at that point. He would be able to manage her symptoms for a while.

A week later, on Labor Day weekend, my eighteen-year-old cat died. She was my child. There were so many things going on, aside from my Mom, including illness-es with other family members, that there was no time to be sad. So, I just moved forward...for the moment.

Over the next few months, it seemed as if each time I had a brief opportunity to breathe and process what was happening around me, something else would oc-cur. I remember one particular day at work, I was feel-ing I finally had a chance to process all the recent events, and Mom called. The next issue was had arrived. As she was talking, I had this vision of myself in the ocean, drowning, trying to come up for air. I couldn't breathe. As I reached out of the water, Jesus grabbed my hand. At that moment, God spoke to my heart. My responsibility was to focus on Him. Period. Not on my list of things to do, or what I needed to do on my day off. I was to spend my time with Him each morning, focus on Him, and He would give me what I needed for the day.

By this point, I was really behind schedule at work and trying desperately to reign in the tears. I really needed a moment to re-group but didn't have the time, as a patient was waiting for me in my room. To shorten the story, that patient walked out on me. In twenty-some years, I have never had a patient walk out. She didn't like my attitude. All I needed was a moment for a deep breath and to cry but that is not part of a hygienist's schedule. God did provide an opportunity for me to apologize and explain the situation to her a month or so later and she accepted my apology. And fortunately, my boss was understanding and didn't fire me.

When life his hitting you from both sides, take a moment to breath and re-group. Focus on God and seek His counsel each day on how to proceed. Don't ask, "What else is going to happen?" Something usually does when you ask. You are inviting it in by asking. Don't worry about tomorrow, or next week, or what "to-do list" you start for your day off. Seek God and let Him order your steps for each day. It is significantly less stressful. I think that was one of, if not the biggest, lessons I learned from all this. And it changed me. It changed the way I viewed and dealt with the remainder of my mother's illness.

When doubts filled my mind, your comfort gave me
renewed hope and cheer.
Psalm 94:19

Life Changing Encounter

*And we know that God causes everything to work together
for the good of those who love God and are called according to
his purpose for them.*

Romans 8:28

My mother firmly believed God was going to heal
her, and she was not going to have a liver transplant.
She was very verbal about this with her doctors as well.
But she was a compliant patient and followed all instructions and was at every appointment on time, if
not early. And I can assure you, there were many, many
appointments.

Dr. G. was able to manage her symptoms well and
keep things controlled, for the most part. This helped
with her cognitive functioning and memory some too.
It was important to help the body work as properly as

possible to keep the toxins down. Having your liver not function properly affects everything in your body.

Getting your name on a transplant list is also not as easy as it sounds. There is a process, and the sickest person jumps to the head of the line. Finally, she did make it onto the list. After that, it is just a matter of waiting.

Mom had surrendered her life to God many years prior to this. But during this time of waiting, she really dove into His Word. She firmly believed in His healing, without a transplant. Occasionally, a situation arose that landed her in the hospital. She would the doctors: "It's okay, this is just a little sidestep. He will still heal me. God is in control."

One day we were chatting, and she was very adamant about not needing the transplant and receiving healing. I finally mentioned to her the possibility of God bringing her healing through the transplant, of leaving the method up to Him. A transplant may be how He wants to bring her healing. She became very quiet. I just wanted her to be open to what God wanted to do.

Dr. G. called me sometime in January 2011 to inform me her kidneys were becoming an issue. She would most likely need a kidney transplant in addition to the liver transplant. Her kidneys were no longer functioning properly because of the failing liver. Basically, she was becoming sicker. They were hoping to do a liver and kidney transplant at the same time from the same donor. Dr. G. informed Mom of this too.

Mom was coming to terms with the need for transplant surgery. She realized this might be God's method of bringing her healing. It is His choice. She continued to dive into His Word. She was frustrated she couldn't remember things. I think that was difficult for my now-stepdad too. Mom had always been smart and had a good memory. Now he had to remember things for her.

As the months went on, I could tell her body was struggling to keep up. Simple things were becoming difficult for her. She was extremely tired, not hungry, and felt nauseous all the time. I felt her body was not managing as well as it was initially. In February, I called my brother to inform him I didn't think Mom would make it to August, the one-year mark. If he had anything he needed to say to her, he needed to say it very soon. I wasn't certain he would have the chance if he waited. Otherwise, we were just waiting. Waiting for that call...

My mom and stepdad were just dating during her illness. He was an answer to prayer, we could not have managed all the doctor visits and recovery without him. They were going to be married. Never did my mom expect, at one of the happiest moments of her life, to be told she had a year to live without a liver and kidney transplant. Shattered dreams. She was looking forward to marriage and travel. Now her life was filled with uncertainty, fogginess in her thinking, and so many doctor appointments. There wasn't time for anything else. Aside from the fact she was too exhausted to do anything, what if "the call" came? She couldn't travel far from home anyway. And he didn't expect the woman he loved to have a life-threatening illness, with an end date at that. Mom kept trying to give him an out, this wasn't what he signed up for. But he said he wasn't going anywhere. Shattered dreams. Often, they would have "dates" after her doctor visits if she was up to it and go out to lunch or something, appreciating the little things in life.

I often reminded all three of us that mom's situation is not a surprise to God, and He had it all under control. We need to trust Him.

"The call" came Sunday, May 22, 2011. Monday, May 23 mom spent fourteen hours in surgery receiving a liver and kidney transplant. It's crazy, but I felt God had given me peace, an assurance, that everything was going to be fine.

The road to recovery was not an easy one. Her lung collapsed the next morning, day two. The new kidney didn't seem to be responding well. They went back into surgery to evaluate and decided to keep her in a comatose state for the next twenty-four hours. On day three she was back in surgery to remove the non-functioning new kidney. It was turning necrotic. She was still on the ventilator and not taken off until day five. She was moved out of ICU and onto the regular transplant floor on day seven. Most are moved out of ICU on day three or day four at the latest.

The high doses of anti-rejection medicines made her like Dr. Jekyll and Mr. Hyde. I never knew what version of my mom I was going to get when I stopped by or called. Finally, I asked the head nurse about this, she wasn't acting at all like my mother. She explained it was due to the medicine and would improve as the doses were decreased. Whew!

Mom spent a total of twenty-eight days in the hospital and months recovering at home after. She experienced a serious rejection eight months later, then she finally seemed to be on the mend. Her own kidney perked up, temporarily. Other than frequent lab work, it was just a matter of her body healing.

But here is the amazing thing that came out of all this: After mom came home from the hospital, she told me she died while she was on the table. She met Jesus, sat with Him, and didn't want to come back here. She never thought she would be willing or ready to leave my brother and I, but she didn't want to come back here. But He told her it wasn't her time; He had work for her to do. How amazing is that?!

There was one small detail I had not shared with my mom until three years later, just before her second kidney transplant. I didn't feel it was time until then. But she had flat-lined on the table. The doctors had to shock her to re-start her heart again. I didn't tell anyone but my husband, until three years later. And then she came out of surgery telling us she had met Jesus. Wow.

It's a crazy thing having an organ transplant. Jesus died for her and gave her new spiritual life. And the loss of someone else's life allowed her to continue to live in this life physically. It is a lot to cope with.

My mom tells everyone about Jesus—in the grocery store, the shoe store… Having surgery? She is the girl you want to talk to. I am blown away at how God has changed her life and given her boldness to tell others about Him. And He has given her the ability to see and seize those opportunities. Who knew?

God knew. It was His plan. God allowed her to go through that situation so she would have a life changing encounter with Him! In November 2012 she and my stepdad were married. Her second kidney transplant was a success. She said Jesus was right there in the operating room with her, holding her hand. She could feel Him. Now she lives a happy, quiet, married life, telling others about Jesus.

God can truly bring good out of any situation when we keep our focus on Him and surrender our will to His. He causes *everything*, all our shattered pieces, our brokenness, our pain, "to work together for good of those who love God and are called according to His purpose for them."

And so, Lord, where do I put my hope?
My only hope is in you.
Psalm 39:7

DAWN M. MITCHELL

Knowing Your
Limits

"The best and most beautiful things in the world
cannot be seen, or touched, but are felt in the heart."
Hellen Keller

Early on, there were so many times that I questioned
our move back to Baltimore in early 2001.Was it really God's timing? Did we hear Him correctly? We often wondered if we would conceive after moving back
home. Crazy thought, huh? All our brothers were having beautiful children, would it now be our turn? We
were a little excited to see what God was going to do.
We were hopeful.

"Hope." What a powerful word. "Hope" enables you to
continue moving forward with confident expectation.

We could see God's hand at work in the moving process. Our home sold very fast, much to our surprise.
We moved in with my mother, bringing three cats and

a very large dog into her townhome. Thankfully, God enabled us to get jobs quickly and we moved into our new home within four months. Although it wasn't in the area we had initially hoped for, we both felt it was the house God had for us.

It was nice being back with family and spending time with our nieces and nephew. As time went by, and we secretly still waited and hoped for our own little blessing, new nieces or nephews were on the way. At that time, it was still challenging for me to be around women who were pregnant—something I so desperately longed for. Fortunately, there were more good days than bad, God had given me so much strength. Yet, when I did have a bad day, there were lots of tears. And it would sometimes hit at odd moments. To this day, I still find it very difficult to attend baby showers. I am happy to send a gift—I just can't bring myself to go. I know my limits.

As you are coming to terms with your shattered dream, you may realize there is something you just can't bring yourself to do because it ends up being too upsetting. I think that is okay but evaluate your motives. Are you truly happy for others involved, and wishing them the best? Is it just too painful, or are you jealous and bitter?

If you are unable to attend a function because the shattering of your dream is still too painful and fresh, yet you wish those involved happiness and blessings, that's one thing. But if you are jealous, angry, and bitter, those feelings must be dealt with. They are not of God, and certainly not part of the abundant life He desires you to live. His desire is for you to live in freedom. Galatians 5:13 states, "For you have been called to live in freedom, my brothers and sisters. But don't use your freedom to satisfy your sinful nature. Instead, use your freedom to serve one another in love."

I had a conversation with my friend, Louise, one day. Her son was in a diving accident and is paralyzed from the neck and shoulders down. As of now, he can breathe on his own but has limited use of his arms—no use of his forearms, wrists, or hands. We are still praying for increased function of his arms and hands, and even that one day he will walk again. Never lose hope. I am a firm believer that God is still in the miracle-working business.

His prom was coming up and he was planning on going. Out of love for him, many of the mothers worked together, going above and beyond, to have the venue changed and have ramps put in so that he could attend. Louise said she thought it was wonderful, but she was not sure he really wanted to go. She felt he was very anxious about going, and the anxiety was heightened by all the effort being made.

The night before prom, he ended up getting sick, and was then unable to attend. Louise said she wondered to herself if the sickness may have been related to his emotions—he seemed to have been relieved that he could not go.

I said, "Why would he want to go? It would be like asking me to go to a baby shower. I'm genuinely happy for the person who is having the baby, but there is nothing I can contribute. I've not been through labor. I haven't had children of my own. I can't join in the talk. I end up feeling anxious prior to going and want to cry long before it's time to leave. Then I have a bunch of emotions to deal with."

"It's the same for your son. I'm sure he is really happy for his classmates, but he can't join in. Prom is not going to be what he has always envisioned. It will only be a reminder of what it isn't for him."

Louise thought that might be exactly what he had been feeling. She also knew he probably felt bad that he appeared ungrateful for the effort being expended on his behalf.

I realize having a miscarriage and not being able to have a child is very, very different from losing your ability to move and walk and the two can hardly be compared. But when dealing with broken dreams, it's okay to know your limits and not intentionally put yourself in situations, or allow others to put you in situations, well-intended as they are, that you know will bring you significant pain and suffering. God doesn't want that. Even athletes are aware of the limits to which they can push their bodies.

I know that baby showers are a bit much for me to handle. Usually, the conversations center around pregnancy, labor, and newborns. I haven't experienced any of that. Listening to the conversation causes my eyes to swell with tears that I must restrain, and a knot forms in my stomach...I have nothing to offer. Baby showers are my limit. For Louise's son, it was prom—and understandably so. Instead of possibly making himself sick with anxiety, he could have simply said he was not comfortable going; or that he wasn't ready to deal with it. Period.

Allowing ourselves to be put in situations because we are concerned about what other people may think, or because we feel we have a responsibility to do a something, isn't healthy. If the other people involved really love us, they will understand. We only need to be concerned about what God thinks and the motives behind the choices we make.

As we go through the healing process and God picks up the shattered pieces and mends us, I have come to realize that sometimes, there remains a tender spot.

That tender spot is a reminder of the pain you felt and helps you see how far you have come in the healing process. Although there is still pain, it enables you to feel thankful for how far God has brought you. It also provides you with an understanding and ability to relate to people going through the discomfort of similar situations. Pain isn't so far from you that you no longer have compassion for someone else.

He comforts us all in our troubles so that we can comfort others. When they are troubled, we will be able to give them the same comfort God has given us.
2 Corinthians 1:4

DAWN M. MITCHELL

Receiving Closure

Make thankfulness your sacrifice to God, and keep the vows
you made to the Most High.
Psalms 50:14

Some of you may be thinking–why get so upset over a miscarriage? In the grand scheme of things, I realize it could be worse. But having children was a dream I'd had since I was a child myself, the loss of that dream is no less painful than someone else's shattered dream. Pain is pain.

I believe life begins at conception. I saw her on the ultrasound. I heard her heartbeat. I even felt her move once, a little flutter. It was the most amazing feeling. To me, that is the day God chose to take her home to be with Him and He allowed her to say goodbye.

One day, I will meet her face to face. David also believed he would see his son again. In 2 Samuel 12:23 he says, "But why should I fast when he is dead? Can I bring him back again? I will go to him one day, but he shall not return to me."

The love that I have for her amazes me. I love her deeply and never had the opportunity to hold her in my arms, to hear her laugh, or dry her tears. I carried her for such a few short weeks and yet remember the flutter of her existence as if it was yesterday.

David Platt said, "There is a unique pain that comes from preparing a place in your heart for a child that never comes." There is so much truth to that statement. There really aren't words to describe it. I love her. I've never met her. She touched my life briefly and left a void where she should be—an area of my heart exclusively for her.

This is the area that misses her. This is the area that wonders what she would have been like. Would she have had John's green eyes or my blue-green eyes? Our blonde hair, or possibly red since John had a red beard? Would she have had John's love and ability for all things mechanical or my love for medicine and health stuff? That is the area of my heart that finds baby showers painfully difficult. I miss her. I will always miss her.

Unlike some others who have struggles with miscarriage or infertility, our story does not end with a beautiful baby. After serious time seeking God, we knew adoption was not the will of God for us. We are all for adoption and have friends who have successfully adopted wonderful children. Each couple must seek His will for their lives in this situation.

We thought for certain God would bless us with a child after we moved back home to Baltimore, close to family. Nope. Years went by. At age thirty-five, after exploratory surgery, I was diagnosed with severe endometriosis and fibroids. I had been having some issues and pain for a few years, so it was nice to have a diagnosis.

But it didn't sound serious, and I didn't fully understand the implications of it initially. I was told I may need a hysterectomy in the future.

"When?"

"We will wait and see."

"Children?"

"We will wait and see."

That seemed to be the answer for everything. We just had to wait for the outcome of treatment. The doctor tried to remove as much of the scar tissue as he could during the surgery, and I tried medication to control symptoms and to help prevent further damage.

John and I were beginning to realize that time was running out for us to have a child. Still seeking God, we considered surrogacy. Either my friend, Gina, or my sister-in-law, Grace, would be a perfect surrogate and we thought it was something both would seriously consider.

I started having more pain. I had switched doctors by this point. I knew a hysterectomy was going to be in my future, but the new doctor gave me options and wanted to wait as long as possible. Well, at thirty-nine, I could wait no longer unless I wanted it to end up being an emergency. I had so much discomfort, at times I could not stand up straight to walk down the hall.

I had seriously mixed emotions. On one hand, all the pain and issues would be over, but so would my chances of having a child. At this point, did I even have a chance of having a child? All those years I had held out hope for God to grant us the child we so desperately desired; because with God, all things are possible. And now I was being told I need a hysterectomy at the age of thirty-nine, removing any slim chance I had of conceiving.

Sometimes God brings blessings in the most amazing ways. Once the surgery was over, I felt as if a weight had been lifted off of me. Relief. Not just for the health issues, but now I knew for certain, our answer was, "No." We would not be having any children in this life. I felt God had shown me mercy. Not only did He heal the health issues and remove the awful monthly visitor, but He had closed the door on my child-bearing ability. I could move forward. It still made me sad at times, but I knew for certain it wasn't going to happen. I had closure.

Although the answer was, "No," I chose to be thankful. I chose to be thankful for the healing He brought to my body through surgery. I chose to be thankful for healing from the physical pain I felt. I chose to be thankful God answered me with certainty that we would not be having children. I chose to be thankful for the strength He had given me. I chose to be thankful for the things He has shown me and taught me through this. And I chose to be thankful for opportunities He gave me to encourage others through my pain. I chose to be thankful for the wonderful husband He has given me.

Have you caught on yet? We need to find the things we can be thankful for, even when we hurt the most.

Be thankful in all circumstances, for this is God's will for you who belong to Christ Jesus.
1 Thessalonians 5:18

DAWN M. MITCHELL

Choose Happiness

"Happiness is a choice."
Joyce Meyer

One of the most profound statements I have ever heard is: "Happiness is a choice." I love Joyce Meyer. She is so straight forward and to the point. This is my favorite quote. When I first heard it, I wrote it on sticky notes and stuck them everywhere. Now I know Joyce Meyer is not the first person to say that happiness is a choice, but when I heard her say it, it stuck with me.

Every day we make choices. Those choices can help lift you up or bring you down. I encourage you to be mindful of the choices you make every day regarding your emotions. It is so easy to become depressed, sad, or hurt because life seems a bit rough. It's difficult to not focus on the problems at hand. Focusing on or worrying about your problems isn't going to get you anywhere.

Happiness is a choice and you must choose to be happy regardless of your circumstances. For years I had allowed my shattered dreams to cause me unhappiness. I could go along my merry way and then stumble into a mother with a newborn and I'd be fighting tears the rest of the day. That newborn was a blessing to his or her mother and I should be happy for her. I had to train myself to be happy despite my circumstances. If I was walking in the will of God for my life, I had no reason to be sad.

It's no different than choosing to be thankful. It's easy to find reasons to be thankful when life is going great but during difficult times, you may have to dig a little. Once you do, it gets easier to find those things to be thankful for. Being thankful helps you focus on the positive, which then causes you to be happy.

Pray over your situation. Surrender it to God. Review scripture. Write down verses and carry them in your pocket so you can re-read them during the day when you need encouragement. This will help you to focus on God instead of your situation, allowing you to choose to be happy and thankful anyway.

For years after I miscarried, I wondered if I did something wrong to cause the loss of my child. *Was it all the years of unhealthy eating? The car accident? The thyroid issues? Was God angry at me? Or worse, was I unworthy of being a mother?*

Satan loves to throw these darts into our thoughts, causing us to think it's all our fault, God is angry at us, we are being punished, or we are unworthy. The list could go on and on. However, the Bible says:

> Finally, believers, whatever is true, whatever is honorable and worthy of respect, whatever is right and confirmed by God's word, whatever is pure and wholesome, whatever is lovely and brings peace, whatever is admirable and of good repute; if there is any excellence, if there is anything worthy of praise, think continually on these things [center your mind on them and implant them in your heart.] The things which you have learned and received and heard and seen in me, practice these things [in daily life], and the God [who is the source] of peace and well-being will be with you.
> Philippians 4: 8-9 (AMP)

God is not angry at you. You are not unworthy. You are His most precious child. Jesus loved you enough to give His life for you. If you made a mistake that contributed to your dreams being shattered, seek His forgiveness, forgive yourself, and move on.

Remember—life happens. Often during difficult times in our lives, we press in to God, and seek His guidance on a much deeper level, more committed than ever. And we learn so much, not just about ourselves, but about His unending love for us, and that He didn't leave us, but was right there with us in the midst of the pain, giving us strength and comfort as we needed it. We become so much closer to our Heavenly Father in ways we might not have otherwise.

Let your roots grow down into him, and let your lives be built on him. Then your faith will grow strong in the truth you were taught, and you will overflow with thankfulness.

Colossians 2:7

DAWN M. MITCHELL

Encouraging Words

Wise words satisfy like a good meal;
the right words bring satisfaction.
Proverbs 18:20

Please choose your words carefully when trying to encourage others going through difficult situations. Think, and pray, before you speak. So often people just want to be helpful, or they want to say something that makes you feel hopeful. But it can backfire if it doesn't come to pass, causing them to doubt you as a friend, or worse, doubt God.

Be mindful about the questions you ask. Recently, a friend of ours found out he would not get the job he had so desired. He spent two years preparing for the position only to be told it would never happen. Someone asked him right after he heard, "So what are you going to do now?" (Yes, people actually do this.) Shortly after, another person asked, "What's next dude?" like it was no big deal. It was a big deal and he was devastated. Initially, he didn't know how he was going to proceed. Such questions are rude, and often asked too early.

When you are with a group of people, it could be a church gathering, a company picnic, a friend's Christmas party, it's common courtesy to make small talk with people you don't know well, if you know them at all. Common questions include: "What area do you live in? Where do you work? What is your position with the company? Do you have any children?"

"Do you have any children?" Early on, I replied that we were trying. Once we realized it wasn't happening quickly, I kept my mouth shut to avoid "helpful tips" and unsolicited advice from people I didn't know well. People would ask us what position we had sex in and say if we had sex in this position or that one, it should help get things where they need to be. Hello, not your business and I don't know you that well. "Will you adopt?" Umm, still too personal. I learned quickly to just say, "We are thinking about it," and move on. I didn't want to discuss it.

Be mindful that your questions are genuine, showing concern and compassion. And, unless you're close friends—not too personal, regardless of the situation.

Early on, friends would say things like: "Forget about it and it will happen." Or, "Oh—you will have one, just give it time." And my favorite (I'm being sarcastic) is, "Adopt and you will get pregnant." Other times, attempting to be helpful, people would tell John and I they had a dream that we conceived and had a child, or God spoke to them that He had not forgotten us, or we were going to have twins at this particular time. People going through difficult times they will cling to those kinds of words with everything in them. Be sure the words you speak are from God, otherwise you are giving them false hope. And believe me, they will cling to those false hopes, but in the end, those empty words will only add to their sorrow.

If someone has spoken words to you, and you are uncertain, ask God to confirm if those words are from Him. I asked Him to confirm if we were going to conceive with twins. He did not confirm those words and we didn't conceive by the time the person had mentioned. Often if words are from God, they will bring a peace or a check within your spirit; and they will come to pass at the proper time.

About 20 years after my miscarriage, Gina, her oldest son Jonathon, and I were watching a movie about a couple who couldn't conceive, and the associated struggles they endured. It was a sad movie and I don't remember much about it. Watching the movie felt awkward and painful to me. I could feel every emotion the couple went through.

As Gina and I talked about the movie the next day, I told her how it was still very painful at times. I don't feel like a mom, and I don't think others consider me a mother because I didn't carry to term, yet I know I have a child in heaven waiting to meet me.

Gina kept debating about saying something. Finally, she said it. She thought I should make a scrapbook and write down everything I thought and felt and include any cards and photographs.

But Gina paused before speaking. She said a quick prayer to be sure that it was of God, not just empty words, and would promote healing.

Gina and I were both surprised that Jonathon, her son, remembered. He was just a little boy then, but he remembered me coming by. He remembers that day. He said they were supposed to do something that day but ended up not doing it so his mom could be there for me. He remembered me crying. He was five years old.

I thought about this for a while. Eventually, I did it. I put together a scrapbook. I journaled how we felt when we found out we were going to have a child, and I included all the congratulatory letters and cards we received. Along with Anna's ultrasound pictures, I included photographs of the carriage, baby blankets, and handmade sweaters—all the things I had waiting for her arrival.

I journaled about the day we found out we were not going to carry to term. I also included a few letters I had written to her, one of which was on what would have been her twentieth birthday.

Words cannot express the release and healing putting together that scrapbook gave me. It gave me something tangible, that proved she had been here. That I felt her, she was real. When a word is from God, it has purpose and it does what it's supposed to do, and it will bring healing. It won't just be empty words.

You may not feel God has helped you, and given you great strength, or helped you to be a light in the area where you feel so weak. But others see it. Others see you trying to plow through, to be strong, and to be happy for those blessed in the area of your sadness.

Recently, I made a baby quilt for Jonathon and his beautiful wife, Amber., They were about to have a baby. Gina told me how touched she was and how much strength it showed that I would even consider making a baby quilt. She knew each stitch was made with love, but painfully so. That is what made me think again that maybe I was to write this book. Maybe God has brought me significantly farther than I thought—and

I am grateful. My desire has always been, if I must go through this, that He, my Lord and Savior, would be glorified in some way. And, that my situation would somehow help bring comfort to others.

"Others see you trying to plow through,
to be strong, and to be happy for those blessed
in the area of your sadness."
Dawn Mitchell

DAWN M. MITCHELL

The Process

"Sometimes the smallest things take up
the most room in your heart."
Winnie the Pooh

Living with shattered dreams is more like a process. Have I arrived yet? No. But I know that I am walking in the life God has planned for me.

And that is what matters. Jeremiah 29:11 states: "'For I know the plans I have for you', says the Lord, 'they are plans for good and not for disaster, to give you a future and a hope.'" I think about those words often, about God having a plan for our lives. When parents of a newborn look at their tiny baby, they have dreams for that child. Dreams of their child becoming a doctor, a lawyer, an accountant, a pastor. Dreams for them to grow up, be healthy, happy, and one day have a family of their own.

Likewise, when God created each of us, I truly believe that he had a plan and a design for each of us. It's more than just coming to know Him through Salvation, but He has a plan for us, "every moment laid out before a single day had passed" (Psalm 139:16). When He created each one of us and looked at us, He had a purpose in mind, something He wanted us to accomplish.

When we walk through our shattered dreams, that is all part of His plan. Nothing happens in our lives that is out of His control, or He hasn't given permission for. If you remember, Satan had to get permission from God before he could test Job. (See Job 1:6-13.) As painful as it is, somewhere along the way there is a purpose in the difficulties we face, whether we know it on this side of eternity or not.

Looking back, I can see the hand of God everywhere. He allowed me to hear Anna's heartbeat, to feel her flutter, to have an ultrasound picture. I believe every life, regardless of length, has a purpose. God's purpose for Anna's brief life was simple. A beating heart. A flutter in the womb. An ultrasound picture. And a slightly swollen abdomen from her growing. Then she was allowed to return to Him.

My Heavenly Father knew how much those things would mean to me. They were tangible evidence that she was here. She existed. And I will meet her one day. Until then, I trust that He tells her about John and me as He rocks her to bed each night.

Often, we can't see or don't realize God is working, until we take time to look back and see how far we have come. It is important to keep our eyes open to other blessings and joys He has brought into our lives, not missing the other ways He has brought happiness and peace to us.

Sometimes in life we will go through a situation, deal with it, and it's over. And then there are times when our dreams are shattered into pieces on the ground and we never really "finish" dealing with them. Yet through the adversity, each situation and struggle we face, God makes us stronger. We learn something and we grow along the way. Have I arrived yet? No. It's about the process.

The process encourages us to lean on and walk more closely with God, the One who gives us comfort and strength. We realize He has not abandoned us. The end result is a closer relationship with our Savior than we may have had otherwise. Maybe, the process isn't such a bad thing after all...

DAWN M. MITCHELL

You saw me before I was born,
Every day of my life was recorded in your book.
Every moment was laid out before
a single day had passed.
Psalm 139:16

Epilogue

Writing this book has been an amazing journey. If you would have told me, not only was I going to write a book, but my best friend would write the Foreword, *and* it would be published by Trilogy Publishing—I would have probably told you that you were crazy. To me, it is an example of how God can bring good and healing out of a painful situation, and open doors at just the right time.

Often, things in life happen that take you down a path you would have never imagined. None of these things are out of God's control or put you beyond His reach. These are sometimes the things that pull us toward Him.

In all my imaginations and dreams for our future, not once did it ever include a life without children. Early on as we sought God, we assumed, we would have children. We believed He would answer, but the answer for the moment was not yet. We had to wait, and trust.

Trust. The thought of trusting can evoke feelings of apprehension, of fear, of not being in control. Trust calls us to surrender. It is difficult to trust when we are hurt, don't understand, or have been let down by other people. Trusting God means believing He has our best interests in mind, and He can work all things out for our good, even in the painful circumstances we didn't see coming.

Amazing things happen and dreams are birthed when we allow God to use us, and our circumstances, to help others and glorify Him. That is one of the benefits of surrendering our will to His—to trusting Him. Trust He will answer your deepest prayer according to what He deems best. Some may say He did not answer our prayer. But I say He did, just not the way we would have chosen. God answered our prayers, but He did so according to His will and purpose for our lives.

As I look back, especially with the miscarriage and infertility, I realized God did not abandon me. He was with me each step of the way. He gave me strength and encouragement when I needed it. He also opened my eyes to see the other blessings He has provided.

Regardless of the battle you are facing, He is with you. He will not abandon you. My prayer for you is that you find encouragement and strength through the words and Scriptures in the pages of this book.

If you have not yet invited Christ into your life, to be your Lord and Savior, I encourage you to do so. He loves you. I spent so many years questioning His love for me, feeling like a disappointment to Him, and wondering why He would ever choose to use me—I'm just...me. But He loves you. I believe He loves each of us as if we were His only child. The capacity of His love for us is so much more than we could ever, ever comprehend. That does not mean we will not face difficult situations or hardships. The Bible says the rain falls on the righteous and the unrighteous alike. "For he gives his sunlight to both the evil and the good, and he sends the rain on the just and the unjust alike" (Matthew 5:45). It does mean He will guide you, open doors at the right time, give you courage and strength. But you need to invite Him in and allow His will, purpose, and plan for you to unfold. Trust Him.

And maybe, at some point, He will use you to bring hope to someone else because you have been where they are.

May God's blessings, love, and strength be with you always.

Dawn

Afterword

Louise and her family have shown tremendous faith, courage, and strength that has reached beyond their family and close friends, to impact the lives of others. Currently, Louise's son, Archer, is attending UPenn, majoring in Engineering and Computer Science. He is managing well, with his parents alternating his 24/7 care, as he continues making his way through incredible barriers. Like the rest of us, he just takes one day at a time. Louise says he has an inner knowing about life and is very wise and kind.

The family believes Archer is alive because of a year of intense communal prayer and God's mercy and divine plan that she believes has yet to fully unfold. I believe the faith, courage, and strength this family has shown has been an inspiration to others. I am thankful to Louise and Archer for allowing me to share our conversation. May God's plan and blessings unfold in their lives.

My mother, Mary, and her husband, Dan, have been married for seven years now. This May will be her eighth year since the liver transplant, and fourth year since her second kidney transplant. She feels she tires more easily than she used to, preventing her from sometimes accomplishing all the things she wants to do. So, it is just one day at a time, one project at a time. She continues to tell others about the goodness of God, despite any challenging circumstances they may be facing.

Trust in the Lord with all your heart;
do not depend on your own understanding.
Seek his will in all you do,
and he will show you which path to take.

Psalm 3: 5-6

DAWN M. MITCHELL

About the Author

Dawn Mitchell resides in Baltimore with her husband and three cats. She is a fulltime Dental Hygienist. Over the years, she has volunteered in various areas of children's ministry, served as a missions treasurer and board secretary. Aside from her cats, sewing, and photography (especially of her cats) she enjoys helping others lay out a plan to pay off debt and experience more financial freedom.

She hopes her debut book, *Shattered Dreams? God Has Not Abandoned You*, will bring her readers comfort and encouragement, and ultimately a closer, more personal relationship with God.

You may contact Ms. Mitchell at:

dawnmitchell236@yahoo.com

or

9613C Harford Road, #189

Baltimore, Maryland 21234

DAWN M. MITCHELL

CPSIA information can be obtained
at www.ICGtesting.com
Printed in the USA
FSHW011255020720
71345FS

9 781647 730383